# How to create a Neonatal Withdrawal Center

# How to create a Neonatal Withdrawal Center

—⁂—

*A New Model of Care for Neonatal Abstinence Syndrome*

Mary Calhoun Brown; Sara Murray, RN;
Rhonda Edmunds, RN; and Sean Loudin, MD

ISBN: 1511864257
ISBN-13: 9781511864251
Library of Congress Control Number: 2015907049
CreateSpace Independent Publishing Platform
North Charleston, South Carolina

# Contents

# Introduction

Our story begins with a newborn's cries that turn to screams and a nurse who cannot find a way to soothe him. Unfortunately, it's a story told far too often in the United States, and the number of infants prenatally exposed to drugs is on the rise everywhere.

Huntington, West Virginia, is the epicenter of this new epidemic. We have eleven times the national average of drug overdoses in our small town of fifty thousand people. We have the largest number of new cases of hepatitis B in the nation and the second-largest number of new cases of hepatitis C. And sadly, along with an addicted population, we have the greatest number of babies born exposed to drugs before birth: one in four. Often the physical need for drugs is what leads women to become pregnant in the first place.

When 25 percent of an infant population is born with withdrawal symptoms, a community begins to take notice, and ours did. First the local hospital created a new, separate twelve-bed unit to alleviate the overcrowding in the neonatal intensive care unit (NICU). Very quickly the twelve-bed unit was filled to capacity, demonstrating an obvious problem.

With more babies than beds, the community came together to create what is now Lily's Place. We started as a faithful handful of concerned citizens, and now we are a national model of care for babies suffering from neonatal abstinence syndrome (NAS) and their parents.

At Lily's Place, we believe in the pursuit of wellness for the entire family, and that includes the addicted parents. We see addiction as a disease, and we work together with families to meet their needs, whether those needs relate to food, clothing, shelter, or addictions. We do the child little good nurturing him through his acute period of withdrawal if we then send him back into an unhealthy environment. We believe that by providing nonjudgmental support to families, we are, indeed, providing for the "least of these," as described in Matthew 25:40.

Our story is one of trial and error—and finally, success. We are licensed as a twelve-bed, stand-alone NAS center, the first one ever. And our goal is to help you respond to the newborn cries and assist in the healing of the prenatally exposed infant. We hope this guide will help you on your journey.

# Building the Board

When creating Lily's Place, a residential treatment facility for NAS babies, we found that having the right heart was the most important component. The IRS requires that a nonprofit board have at least three members. We had many community members who wanted to be on the board, but in the beginning we chose to keep our board as small as possible. With all of the documents that needed to be signed, this decision ended up being a wise one—we had to track down only three people instead of a dozen or more. Having a small board has also assisted in planning board meetings. Finding times to meet was never a challenge, and often we met over breakfast.

Our initial board had a legislator/lawyer ("the Senator"), a registered nurse with twenty-five years of experience in caring for NAS babies ("the Nurse"), and a woman with a ton of time and a heart for the babies ("the Advocate"). We also created a planning committee with carefully chosen community members who meet regularly to help us with community awareness and activities.

The Senator was connected on the state level, helping us make sense of the steps necessary to comply with state code. He also helped navigate the process for us, giving us a path to follow and encouragement as we faced governmental bumps in the road.

The Nurse made absolutely certain that the processes and procedures we created were appropriate for our patients. Her guidance and understanding of the diagnosis from both the babies' and parents' perspectives were valuable. Her contacts within the local hospital systems also helped us build necessary partnerships.

The Advocate was the driving force behind jumping through every governmental hoop, getting donations to fund the building renovation, and pushing for timely responses from everyone.

The board's genesis and the very concept of Lily's Place started out of necessity. Two NICU nurses noticed that the incidence of prenatal drug exposure was increasing dramatically in the West Virginia hospital where they worked. One of the nurses, now the director of nursing at Lily's Place, began researching effective treatments for drug-exposed newborns and ran across a foster home in Kent, Washington. The two nurses packed a bag and took a field trip to the foster home.

Within a week of their return, the Advocate, who had been a volunteer baby cuddler at the same hospital, made contact with the Nurse regarding the higher incidence of NAS infants and the infants' aversion to sensory stimuli. The Nurse began telling the Advocate about her trip out west and the need in Huntington, West Virginia, for a facility that would care for babies in a less stimulating environment.

Neither the Nurse nor the Advocate knew anything about starting a business from scratch, and they knew they would need plenty of help navigating the waters of government regulation and compliance. That's when the Advocate suggested they call the Senator.

The Senator had a long history of supporting children. A law he championed required newborns to receive hearing screenings prior to being discharged from the hospital. Another law he created and the state legislature passed required insurance agencies to pay for necessary care for autistic children and adults in the state. The Advocate had known the Senator for over twenty years, and happened to have his cell phone number in her phone.

Within a few short months of meetings, the Nurse, the Advocate, and the Senator had established a firm resolve to work toward the goal of creating an NAS center in West Virginia. The three of them sat at a small table in a break room at the hospital, and each committed to the project. They mutually decided that the Nurse and a well-respected neonatologist would develop the clinical side of things. The Senator would begin sowing seeds with government regulators and legislators, and the Advocate would begin looking for a building and generate community interest and support.

# Creating Bylaws and Articles of Incorporation

Once we had the board in place and committed to Lily's Place, the Advocate asked a neighbor, who was also an attorney, if he would be interested in doing some pro bono work for Lily's Place. When he learned we were looking for help filing for a 501(c)(3) status, he directed us to an attorney friend in his office who was willing to help. The attorney donated his time to help us create the Lily's Place bylaws and articles of incorporation, directing the Advocate as she prepared the documentation for status as a tax-exempt charity. This was the first of hundreds of examples of the kindness of strangers.

Our attorney produced the following documents, and the board approved them. With both the bylaws and articles of incorporation created, we were ready to register through the West Virginia secretary of state as a corporation.

## Our Bylaws

### Article 1. Purpose
The corporation has been organized to operate exclusively for charitable purposes, including but not limited to the following:

1. Provide medical care to infants suffering from prenatal drug exposure.
2. Offer education and support to families and communities to recognize and manage the needs of substance abused babies.
3. Assist child protective services (CPS) in determining the best placement for infants.
4. Reflect the values of professionalism, respect, confidentiality, and diversity in a nurturing, nonjudgmental environment.

## Article II. Location

The principal office of the corporation, at which the general business of the corporation will be transacted and where the records of the corporation will be kept, will be at such a place in the metropolitan area, state of West Virginia, as may be fixed from time to time by the board of directors.

## Article III. Members

Members of the corporation will consist only of the members of the board of directors.

## Article IV. Board of Directors

Section 1: The number of members of the board of directors of this corporation will be not less than three or more than twelve.

Section 2: Directors will be representative of those who care and wish to support these infants in the Huntington area and will share the mission and goals of the corporation. This corporation is committed to a policy of fair representation on the board of directors, which does not discriminate on the basis of race, physical handicap, sex, color, religion, sexual orientation, or age.

Section 3: Election of new directors or election of current directors to a second term will occur as the first item of business at the annual meeting of the corporation. Directors will be elected by a majority vote of the current directors.

Section 4: The term of each director of the corporation will be two years.

Section 5: When a director is unable to serve for any reason, the board may elect a director to serve for the duration of the unexpired term.

Section 6: Any director may be removed from the board of directors by an affirmative vote of the majority of directors present at an official meeting of the board. Notice of the proposed removal will be given to members with the notice of the meeting. The director involved will be given an opportunity to be present and to be heard at the meeting at which his or her removal is considered.

Section 7: No compensation will be paid to any member of the board of directors for services as a member of the board. By resolution of the board, reasonable expenses may be allowed for attendance at regular and special meetings of the board.

## Article V. Meeting of the Board of Directors

Section 1: An annual meeting of the board of directors will be held in July of each year for the purpose of electing officers and directors. In addition to its annual meeting, the board of directors will hold regular meetings at least four times each calendar year at such place as may be designated in the notice of the meeting.

Section 2: Special meetings of the board of directors may be called at any time by the president of the corporation or, in his or her absence, by the vice-president or upon receipt of a request therefore signed by two or more directors or by a majority of the full-time, permanent paid staff of the corporation.

Section 3: Notice of regular, special, and annual meetings will be mailed at least fourteen days prior to the day such meeting is to be held. Any director of the corporation may make written waiver of notice before, at, or after a meeting. The waiver will be filed with the person who has been designed to act as the secretary of the meeting; this person will enter it in the record of the meeting. Appearance at a meeting is deemed a waiver unless the director attends for the express purpose of asserting the illegality of the meeting.

Section 4: At all meetings of the board of directors, each director present will be entitled to cast one vote on any motion coming before the meeting. The presence of a majority of the membership will constitute a quorum at any meeting.

Section 5: At a meeting at which there is a quorum present, a simple majority affirmative vote of the directors present is required to pass a motion before the board.

Section 6: Proxy voting will be permitted.

## Article VI. Officers

Section 1: The officers of this corporation will be president, vice-president, secretary, treasurer, and such officers with duties as the board prescribes.

Section 2: The officers of the corporation will be elected annually by the members of the board of directors at its annual meeting. Each officer will serve two-year terms.

Section 3: Any officer may be removed with or without cause by the board of directors by a vote of a majority of all of the board members. The matter of removal may be acted upon at any meeting of the board, provided that the notice of intention to consider said removal has been given to each board member and to the officer affected at least seven days previously.

Section 4: A vacancy in any office may be filled by a majority vote of the board of directors for the unexpired portion of the term.

Section 5: The president will be the chief executive officer of the corporation. It will be the duty of the president to reside at all meetings of the board of directors and to have general supervision of the affairs of the corporation. He or she will execute on behalf of the corporation all contracts, deeds, conveyances, and other instruments in writing that may be required or authorized by the board of directors for the proper and necessary transaction of the business of the corporation.

Section 6: It will be the duty of the vice-president to act in the absence or disability of the president and to perform such other duties as may be assigned to him or her by the president of the board. In the absence of the president, the execution by the vice-president on behalf of the corporation of any instrument will have the same force and effect as if it were executed on behalf of the corporation by the president.

Section 7: The secretary will be responsible for keeping the corporate records. He or she will give or cause to be given all notices of meetings of the board of directors and all other notices required by law or by these bylaws. The secretary will be the custodian of all books, correspondence, and paper relating to the business of the corporation, except those of the treasurer. The secretary will present at each annual meeting of the board of directors a full report of the transactions and affairs of the corporation for the preceding year and will also prepare and present to the board of directors such other reports as it may desire and request at such time or times as it may designate. The board of directors at its discretion may elect an assistant secretary, not necessarily a member of the board of directors, who will perform the duties and assume the responsibilities of the secretary as above set forth under the general direction of the secretary or president.

Section 8: The treasurer will have general charge of finances of the corporation. When necessary and proper, he or she will endorse on behalf of the corporation all checks, drafts, notes, and other obligations and evidences of the payment of money to the corporation or coming into his or her possession, in such bank or banks as may be selected by the board of directors. He or she will deposit the same, together with all other funds of the corporation coming into his or her possession, and will keep full and accurate account of all receipts and disbursements of the corporation in books belonging to the corporation, which will be open at all times to the inspection of the board of directors. He or she will present to the board of directors at its annual meeting his or her report as treasurer of the corporation and will from time to time make such other reports to the board of directors as it may require.

Section 9: Any officer of the corporation, in addition to the powers conferred upon him or her by these bylaws, will have such additional powers and perform such additional duties as may be prescribed from time to time by said board.

## Article VII. Committees

Section 1: The board of directors may designate one or more ad hoc committees, each of which will consist of at least one committee chair and two or more committee members. Committee members may be members of the board of directors, members of the corporation, or other interested individuals. The chair of the committee will be appointed by the president of the organization who will act with the board's approval. After consultation with the committee chair, the president of the organization will appoint committee members. The studies, findings, and recommendations of all committees will be reported to the board of directors for consideration and action, except as otherwise ordered by the board of directors. Committees may adopt such rules for the conduct of business as are appropriate and as are not inconsistent with these bylaws, the articles of incorporation, or state law.

Section 2: The board of directors will have the following standing committees.

Executive Committee: This committee will be chaired by the president of the corporation and will consist of all other officers of the corporation and the chairs of all other committees. This committee will serve as the central planning group for the organization and as an advisory group to the executive director. It also will have full authority to act for the board in managing the affairs of the corporation during the intervals between meetings of the board.

Budget and Finance: This committee will be chaired by the treasurer and will consist of two to five members appointed by the president to one-year terms. This committee will oversee and monitor the fiscal operations of the organization, develop an annual budget for recommendation by the board, and develop and assist in the implementation of a funding strategy for the corporation.

## Article VIII. Miscellaneous

Section 1: The corporation will have the power to indemnify and hold harmless any director, officer, or employee from any suit, damage, claim, judgment, or liability arising out of, or asserted to arise out of, conduct of such person in his or her capacity as a director, officer, or employee (except in cases involving willful misconduct). The corporation will have the power to purchase or procure insurance for such purposes.

Section 2: The board of directors may authorize any officer or officers, agent or agents of the corporation, in addition to the officers so authorized by these laws, to enter into any contract or execute and deliver any instrument in the name of, and on behalf of, the corporation. Such authority may be general or confined to specific instances.

Section 3: All checks, drafts, and other orders for payment of funds will be signed by such officers or such other persons as the board of directors may from time to time designate. All documents will require two such signatures, at least one of which must be that of a member of the board of directors and the other may be of the executive director.

Section 4: The corporation will keep correct and complete books and records of accounts and will also keep minutes of the proceedings of its members, board of directors, and committees having any of the authority of the board of directors; and it will keep at the registered or principal office a record giving the names and addresses of the members entitled to vote. All books and records of the corporation may be inspected by any member or by his or her agent or attorney for any proper purpose at any reasonable time.

Section 5: The fiscal year of the corporation will be July 1 through June 30.

## Article IX. Amendments

The board of directors may amend these bylaws to include or omit any provision that it could lawfully include or omit at the time the amendment is made. Upon written notice of at least thirty days, any number of amendments or an entire revision of the bylaws may be submitted and voted upon at a single meeting of the board of directors and will be adopted at such meeting upon receiving a two-thirds vote of the members of the board of directors.

## Article X. Dissolution

Upon the dissolution of the corporation and after the payment or the provision for the payment of all the liabilities of the corporation, the board of directors will dispose of all of the assets of the corporation exclusively for the purposes of the corporation or to the organizations that are then qualified as tax-exempt organizations under section 501(c)(3) of the Internal Revenue code. Any assets not so disposed of will be disposed of by a court of jurisdiction in the county in which the principal office of the corporation is located.

# Our Articles of Incorporation

**ARTICLES OF INCORPORATION**

**OF**

**LILY'S PLACE, INC.**

Pursuant to §31E-10-1006 of the West Virginia Nonprofit Corporation Act, **Lily's Place, Inc.**, a West Virginia corporation, adopts the following Articles of Incorporation:

**FIRST:** The name of the corporation is **Lily's Place, Inc.** (the "Corporation").

**SECOND:** The principal office address of the Corporation is 250 Xxxxxxxxx Xxxxx, xxxxxxxxxxxx, xxxxxxxxxxxxx, xxxxxxxxxxxxx, xxxxxx.

**THIRD:** The mailing address of the Corporation is P.O. Box 2, Huntington, West Virginia 25706.

**FOURTH:** The physical address of the principal place of business in West Xxxxx, xxxxxxxxxxxx, xxxxxxxxxxxxx, xxxxxxxxxxxxx, xxxxxx. xxxxxx, xxxxx, xxxxxxxxxxxxx.

**FIFTH:** The name and address of the person to whom notice of process may be sent is Roy F. Layman, Campbell Woods, PLLC, 1002 Third Avenue, P.O. Box 1835, Huntington, West Virginia 25719.

**SIXTH:** The Corporation is organized as a non-profit, non-stock corporation.

**SEVENTH:** The Corporation shall have no members.

**EIGHTH:** The existence of the Corporation is to be perpetual.

**NINTH:** The Corporation is formed for the purposes of conducting an business which may be conducted by a non-profit corporation in the State of West Virginia which is consistent with exemption under Section 501(c)(3) of the Internal Revenue Code of 1986, as amended (the "Code", which shall include any subsequent corresponding Code of Federal tax law). The Corporation

Articles of Incorporation page 1

14

is organized and at all times hereafter shall be operated exclusively for charitable and educational purposes, within the meaning of § 501(c)(3) of the Code, including for such purposes, the making of distributions to organizations that qualify as exempt organizations under § 501(c)(3) of the Code. Without limiting the generality of the forgoing, the general purposes of the Corporation are to provide medical care to infants suffering from prenatal drug or substance abuse exposure and to offer education and support services to families and communities to help recognize and manage the needs of infants suffering from drug and substance abuse.

TENTH: No part of the net earnings of the Corporation shall inure to the benefit of, or be distributable to its members, trustees, officers, or other private persons, except that the Corporation shall be authorized and empowered to pay reasonable compensation for services rendered and to make payments and distributions in furtherance of the purposes set forth in Article Seventh hereof. No substantial part of the activities of the Corporation shall be the carrying on of propaganda, or otherwise attempting to influence legislation, and the Corporation shall not participate in, or intervene in (including publishing or distribution of statements) any political campaign on behalf of or in opposition to any candidate for public office. Notwithstanding any other provisions of these Articles, the Corporation shall not carry on any other activities not permitted to be carried on (a) by a corporation exempt from federal income tax under section 501(c)(3) of the Code, or (b) by a corporation, contributions to which are deductible under section 170(c)(2) of the Code.

ELEVENTH: Upon the dissolution of the Corporation, assets shall be distributed for one or more exempt purposes within the meaning of section 501(c)(3) of the Code, or shall be distributed to the federal government, or to a state or local government, for a public purpose. Any such assets not so disposed of shall be disposed of by a Court of Competent Jurisdiction of the county in which the principal office of the Corporation is then located, exclusively for such purposes or to such organization or organizations, as said Court shall determine, which are organized and operated exclusively for such purposes.

Articles of Incorporation page 2

**TWELFTH:** The names and addresses of the incorporators are:

| Name | Address | City/State/Zip |
|------|---------|----------------|
| Mary Calhoun Brown | Xxxxxxxxxxxxxxxxxx | Huntington, WV 25701 |
| Sara Murray | Xxxxxxxxxxxx | Milton, WV 25541 |
| Evan H. Jenkins | Xxxxxxxxxxxxxxxx | Huntington, WV 25701 |

**THIRTEENTH:** The contact person to reach in case there is a problem with this filing is:

Roy F. Layman, Esquire
Campbell Woods, PLLC
1002 Third Avenue
P. O. Box 1835
Huntington, West Virginia    25719
(304) 529-2391
rlayman@campbellwoods.com

**IN WITNESS WHEREOF,** witness the signatures of the Incorporators as of this 28th day of February, 2011.

Mary Calhoun Brown

This instrument prepared by:
Roy F. Layman, Esquire
Campbell Woods, PLLC
1002 Third Avenue
P. O. Box 1835
Huntington, West Virginia    25719
(304) 529-2391

Articles of Incorporation page 3

# Applying for 501(c)(3) Status

The first step toward obtaining our 501(c)(3) status was to apply for a Federal Employee Identification Number (FEIN). The process is not difficult and can be completed online at http://www.irs.gov/Businesses/Small-Businesses-&-Self-Employed/Apply-for-an-Employer-Identification-Number-%28EIN%29-Online. Please note that a D-U-N-S number is also required; instructions on how to obtain one can be found here: http://www.sba.gov/content/getting-d-u-n-s-number.

Our local lawyer once again provided guidance for filling out the 501(c)(3) paperwork. The appropriate form is IRS Form 1023, which can be downloaded from here: http://www.irs.gov/pub/irs-pdf/f1023. pdf. At first we used the Advocate's home address for important documents because she was working from her home. We recommend getting a post office box early on, however, to avoid receiving business information at a home address.

We incorporated our business through the West Virginia secretary of state's office. We needed our bylaws and articles of incorporation to complete this part. The process was not difficult, and the form is available online for West Virginia corporations at http://www.sos.wv.gov/business-licensing/forms/Documents/Corporation/cd-1.pdf. It is important to hold onto those bylaws, storing a copy of them in the supporting documents.

We created a conflict of interest policy, as required by the IRS for a 501(c)(3). Little did we know how great we would become at policies writing. The state license required stacks of policies, but we will cover that later. We also created a whistleblower policy at the same time. Templates of these two necessary policies are easily found online.

The next step was to create a narrative that explained what we planned to do. There are several components to this narrative, including "Who We Are," "Who We Serve," "Mission Statement," "Duration of Care," and "Reasons for Lily's Place." This particular narrative has been very valuable to us as we continue to build our organization. Our suggestion is to take great care when developing it. We have even used ours as the cornerstone of our business plan, the details of which will be covered in another section.

The hardest part of the 501(c)(3) application was creating a budget for an organization that did not yet exist. We really fretted over that section, but our attorney assured us that the IRS was looking for a general idea, not firm numbers, so we used the information available to us and estimated what our first-, second-, and third-year budgets would be.

As for the actual application form, we strongly suggest you get help from an attorney. Lily's Place is classified as a hospital under section 1 of the application, although according to the state's classification system we are under behavioral health. Because the care of NAS infants outside of hospitals is brand new with Lily's Place, we have had to find ways to fit into already-existing designations as far as the government goes. For example, our city government classifies us as a nursing home, and that classification does make sense given that our patients are here 24/7, require around-the-clock nursing care and medication, and are nonambulatory. In working with our state legislature, we have been able to establish a separate NAS center designation within the state of West Virginia, which will be signed into law at the time this booklet is published.

# We were required to fill out Schedule C of Form 1023. See below.

| Form 1023 (Rev. 6-2006) | Name: Lily's Place, Inc. | EIN: 46 – 2235123 | Page 16 |
|---|---|---|---|

## Schedule C. Hospitals and Medical Research Organizations

| | | |
|---|---|---|
| Check the box if you are a **hospital**. See the instructions for a definition of the term "hospital," which includes an organization whose principal purpose or function is providing **hospital** or **medical care**. Complete Section I below. | | ☑ |
| Check the box if you are a **medical research organization** operated in conjunction with a hospital. See the instructions for a definition of the term "medical research organization," which refers to an organization whose principal purpose or function is medical research and which is directly engaged in the continuous active conduct of medical research in conjunction with a hospital. Complete Section II. | | ☐ |

### Section I    Hospitals

| | | | |
|---|---|---|---|
| 1a | Are all the doctors in the community eligible for staff privileges? If "No," give the reasons why and explain how the medical staff is selected. | ☐ Yes | ☑ No |
| 2a | Do you or will you provide medical services to all individuals in your community who can pay for themselves or have private health insurance? If "No," explain. | ☐ Yes | ☑ No |
| b | Do you or will you provide medical services to all individuals in your community who participate in Medicare? If "No," explain. | ☐ Yes | ☑ No |
| c | Do you or will you provide medical services to all individuals in your community who participate in Medicaid? If "No," explain. | ☐ Yes | ☑ No |
| 3a | Do you or will you require persons covered by Medicare or Medicaid to pay a deposit before receiving services? If "Yes," explain. | ☐ Yes | ☑ No |
| b | Does the same deposit requirement, if any, apply to all other patients? If "No," explain. | ☑ Yes | ☐ No |
| 4a | Do you or will you maintain a full-time emergency room? If "No," explain why you do not maintain a full-time emergency room. Also, describe any emergency services that you provide. | ☐ Yes | ☑ No |
| b | Do you have a policy on providing emergency services to persons without apparent means to pay? If "Yes," provide a copy of the policy. | ☐ Yes | ☑ No |
| c | Do you have any arrangements with police, fire, and voluntary ambulance services for the delivery or admission of emergency cases? If "Yes," describe the arrangements, including whether they are written or oral agreements. If written, submit copies of all such agreements. | ☐ Yes | ☑ No |
| 5a | Do you provide for a portion of your services and facilities to be used for charity patients? If "Yes," answer 5b through 5e. | ☐ Yes | ☑ No |
| b | Explain your policy regarding charity cases, including how you distinguish between charity care and bad debts. Submit a copy of your written policy. | | |
| c | Provide data on your past experience in admitting charity patients, including amounts you expend for treating charity care patients and types of services you provide to charity care patients. | | |
| d | Describe any arrangements you have with federal, state, or local governments or government agencies for paying for the cost of treating charity care patients. Submit copies of any written agreements. | | |
| e | Do you provide services on a sliding fee schedule depending on financial ability to pay? If "Yes," submit your sliding fee schedule. | ☐ Yes | ☐ No |
| 6a | Do you or will you carry on a formal program of medical training or medical research? If "Yes," describe such programs, including the type of programs offered, the scope of such programs, and affiliations with other hospitals or medical care providers with which you carry on the medical training or research programs. | ☑ Yes | ☐ No |
| b | Do you or will you carry on a formal program of community education? If "Yes," describe such programs, including the type of programs offered, the scope of such programs, and affiliation with other hospitals or medical care providers with which you offer community education programs. | ☑ Yes | ☐ No |
| 7 | Do you or will you provide office space to physicians carrying on their own medical practices? If "Yes," describe the criteria for who may use the space, explain the means used to determine that you are paid at least fair market value, and submit representative lease agreements. | ☐ Yes | ☑ No |
| 8 | Is your board of directors comprised of a majority of individuals who are representative of the community you serve? Include a list of each board member's name and business, financial, or professional relationship with the hospital. Also, identify each board member who is representative of the community and describe how that individual is a community representative. | ☑ Yes | ☐ No |
| 9 | Do you participate in any joint ventures? If "Yes," state your ownership percentage in each joint venture, list your investment in each joint venture, describe the tax status of other participants in each joint venture (including whether they are section 501(c)(3) organizations), describe the activities of each joint venture, describe how you exercise control over the activities of each joint venture, and describe how each joint venture furthers your exempt purposes. Also, submit copies of all agreements. | ☐ Yes | ☑ No |

**Note.** Make sure your answer is consistent with the information provided in Part VIII, line 8.

Form **1023** (Rev. 6-2006)

Schedule C

| Form 1023 (Rev. 6-2006) | Name: Lily's Place, Inc. | EIN: 46 – 2235123 | Page 17 |
|---|---|---|---|

**Schedule C. Hospitals and Medical Research Organizations** *(Continued)*

**Section I   Hospitals** *(Continued)*

10  Do you or will you manage your activities or facilities through your own employees or volunteers? If "No," attach a statement describing the activities that will be managed by others, the names of the persons or organizations that manage or will manage your activities or facilities, and how these managers were or will be selected. Also, submit copies of any contracts, proposed contracts, or other agreements regarding the provision of management services for your activities or facilities. Explain how the terms of any contracts or other agreements were or will be negotiated, and explain how you determine you will pay no more than fair market value for services.
☑ Yes  ☐ No

Note. Answer "Yes" if you do manage or intend to manage your programs through your own employees or by using volunteers. Answer "No" if you engage or intend to engage a separate organization or independent contractor. Make sure your answer is consistent with the information provided in Part VIII, line 7b.

11  Do you or will you offer recruitment incentives to physicians? If "Yes," describe your recruitment incentives and attach copies of all written recruitment incentive policies.  ☐ Yes  ☑ No

12  Do you or will you lease equipment, assets, or office space from physicians who have a financial or professional relationship with you? If "Yes," explain how you establish a fair market value for the lease.  ☐ Yes  ☑ No

13  Have you purchased medical practices, ambulatory surgery centers, or other business assets from physicians or other persons with whom you have a business relationship, aside from the purchase? If "Yes," submit a copy of each purchase and sales contract and describe how you arrived at fair market value, including copies of appraisals.  ☐ Yes  ☑ No

14  Have you adopted a **conflict of interest policy** consistent with the sample health care organization conflict of interest policy in Appendix A of the instructions? If "Yes," submit a copy of the policy and explain how the policy has been adopted, such as by resolution of your governing board. If "No," explain how you will avoid any conflicts of interest in your business dealings.  ☑ Yes  ☐ No

**Section II   Medical Research Organizations**

1  Name the hospitals with which you have a relationship and describe the relationship. Attach copies of written agreements with each hospital that demonstrate continuing relationships between you and the hospital(s).

2  Attach a schedule describing your present and proposed activities for the direct conduct of medical research; describe the nature of the activities, and the amount of money that has been or will be spent in carrying them out.

3  Attach a schedule of assets showing their fair market value and the portion of your assets directly devoted to medical research.

Form **1023** (Rev. 6-2006)

Schedule C Continued

After submitting your 501(c)(3) application to the IRS, you simply wait for a letter of determination, which will tell you if you have been approved for tax-exempt status or if more information is required. Once you have been approved, you use your FEIN as your tax-exempt number.

# Finding a Facility and Performing Renovations

While you await your IRS determination letter, you can use your time to find a building. (We were blessed to find a woman who wanted to donate her building to us.) The best way to go about this is to ask everyone you know to keep an eye out for potential donors. It's best to find a one-story building, and it really helps if it already has a sprinkler system, as those run in the tens of thousands of dollars. Ours cost $50,000 for our 7,250-square-foot building. Local attorneys and realtors often know of business properties that have been on the market for years. Our building was a podiatrist's office, and the doctor's widow tried for three years to sell it before deciding to donate it to us. Unless you have deep pockets, a donated building is the way to go.

Holding hands in prayer
Our donated building, located at 1320 Seventh
Avenue in Huntington, West Virginia

The next step is to get the building ready for the necessary city inspections. We started by cleaning everything, floor to ceiling.

Brandi Davis volunteers her time cleaning

Teens cleaning out cabinets

Once we removed the trash and everything smelled great, we invited the city officials to come visit and tell us what we needed to do to receive our certificate of occupancy and our business license through the city of Huntington.

First we needed to be rezoned within the city. We petitioned the city zoning board of appeals to allow us to become a "pediatric addiction recovery center or nursing home," and we also appealed to allow for us to construct a fence with barbed wire around the back for added security. At the zoning board meeting, we stood before the officials and answered questions from them and from concerned citizens. We were unanimously approved on both requests.

We made appointments with the city's building inspector, the plumbing inspector, the electrical inspector, the licensing and tax inspector, the health department, and the fire marshal. The structural inspector passed us right away. The plumbing inspector required we install backflow devices on our waterlines, which we did, and we received a thumbs-up from them about a week later. The electrical inspector found half a dozen small things, and a local electrician donated his time to correct what needed changed. The licensing and tax inspector had a simple process for approval, so that was good. We had a good donation base at that time through our social media, which we will discuss later.

The fire marshal and a new sprinkler system stood between us and our business license. As it turns out, we needed to be licensed through a state agency; therefore, we fell under more stringent fire codes. We used a grant from the state of West Virginia through the Cabell County Family Resource Network to pay for the many fire code upgrades needed. We had to build a one-hour smoke partition from ceiling to floor, install a comprehensive sprinkler system, install additional vents in the mechanical rooms, and make dozens of minor adjustments to doors, exits, and hallways to ensure compliance. This paragraph does not do justice to the amount of work necessary to obtain a certificate of occupancy from the state fire marshal. It was a big deal. Expensive. But it was worth it because we know beyond the shadow of a doubt that our patients are safe at Lily's Place.

Electrical work          HVAC work

Jackhammering floors for the sprinkler system

At the same time, we asked members of our community to sponsor rooms and to help with improving the exterior of our building. Sixteen nurseries were quickly adopted, and folks worked tirelessly to make our rooms the most beautiful places to recover. All were created at zero cost to us. The community provided everything from diapers to rocking chairs to paint. A Boy Scout adopted the front of our building for his Eagle Scout project. Students from across the tristate area volunteered their time to help paint, clean, and move furniture for us. Recovering addicts from the Healing Place painted and helped unload heavy equipment. Words cannot describe the huge volunteer effort to prepare the building for babies, so we are including a few more photographs.

Local sign company donated our sign.

White picket fence goes in.

Volunteer missionaries paint exterior.    The rose bushes and lilies are planted.

Even the little ones
chipped in to help.

Donated drywall is delivered for the smoke partition.

Painting the interior with paint donated by Sherwin Williams

Exterior painting

Teens lending a hand

A volunteer preparing
her room for babies

A church group donating diapers

The roses and fence are in.

A single occupancy nursery

A double occupancy nursery

The fence going up out back

The Optimist Club
replacing all our lights

College students helping move in our lockers

Even the smallest lending a hand

First Lady Joanne Tomblin at the ribbon-cutting ceremony;
the building is finally able to welcome babies.

Welcoming our staff

One of our sweet graduates

# Obtaining a Certificate of Need

Depending on how your state chooses to license you, your organization may need a certificate of need (CON). In West Virginia, certificates of need are the responsibility of the Health Care Authority. The Health Care Authority's goals are to "control health care costs, improve the quality and efficiency of the health care system, encourage collaboration, and develop a system of health care delivery that makes health services available to all residents of West Virginia." The CON program is one way they meet these goals.

In the case of Lily's Place, we were initially under the impression that we would need a certificate of need, which we applied for, and all signs pointed to CON approval from the Health Care Authority. During the public comment period, a local hospital stepped in with its attorneys to stop our progress toward opening. However, because we work with substance abuse, the WV Department of Health and Human Resources helped us pursue a behavioral health license, and we were able to circumvent the CON process.

The CON process can be lengthy, so check with your state's regulatory agencies early in the process of creating an NAS center. As state law changes and new laws are passed, the team at Lily's Place may have to apply for a CON, but we feel certain that no hindrances will block our progress moving forward.

# Staffing

Your staff will be your greatest asset, so you need to keep a few character traits in mind when you hire people. A heart for drug-exposed newborns is the most important trait to look for in an employee. At Lily's Place we have several skilled nurses who took a pay cut to work here. They recognize the value of our work beyond what they bring home in a paycheck every week, and they truly feel that they are providing a necessary service to children in need.

A calm spirit is the second valuable trait to look for. A high-energy person or someone who is always in motion may be an asset to some offices, but babies respond best to nurses and caregivers who can take a deep breath at the door and focus their minds and spirits on the infants in front of them. Busy-bee employees are best left to the front office and away from the patients.

The third trait to look for is someone with a quiet voice. Some people are just loud, and if your goal is to create a low-stimulus environment, you need to look for low-stimulus people.

The final character trait to look for is the ability to maintain professional distance with the parents while still having a compassionate demeanor. We love the parents, and we want to help them get better, but professional distance protects employees and their families from too much involvement.

When staffing your facility, remember to be aware of the rules and regulations involved in dispensing medicine. For example, you will need to have at least two registered nurses in the facility at all times when dispensing any Schedule II narcotic. Additionally, your state will have minimum requirements for child-to-staff ratios, and you must be compliant with those ratios. We maintain a ratio of two patients to one staff member, which is actually a better ratio than our state requires, and with our wonderful volunteers, that ratio gets even better—at a one-to-one ratio when necessary.

No doubt staff salaries will be your greatest expense, but it is important to remember that the comfort and safety of each child is paramount.

In addition to a full staff of registered nurses, we employ patient-care assistants who are either certified nursing assistants (CNAs) or certified medical assistants (CMAs) to help each registered nurse with her caseload.

Our management team includes an executive director, a director of nursing (head nurse), and a designated social worker. Support staff includes a secretary and a security guard.

# Recruiting Volunteers

Volunteers are an integral part of a community-based facility for drug-exposed babies. We rely on our volunteers for everything. Since the early days of organizing Lily's Place, we have utilized volunteers to clean, paint, raise awareness, and decorate nurseries. Hundreds of selfless people have given time, energy, and talents to build something from nothing. No matter who the volunteers are or what their level of mobility is, there are tasks to match every skill and ability.

Many businesses and individuals have had baby showers for us. Still others plan benefit events, mop and dust our building, plant flowers outside, and answer phones. The best job, of course, is being a cuddler. Our cuddlers are available and ready to calm a crying baby or lend an ear to a mother.

Our state requires that we treat volunteers the same way we treat employees. They must undergo a rigorous background check process and formal training. They are responsible for reading and understanding our policies handbook, and they are required to be immunized and to have current TB test results and proof of having received hepatitis B vaccinations.

Our volunteers are scheduled, just as the staff members are scheduled, and they are expected to complete assigned tasks while they are here. We think it's the best volunteer gig in town.

# Training

Prior to employment or volunteering, all staff must take a forty-six-point training session, which includes therapeutic handling techniques. A multidisciplinary team of experts walks new volunteers and employees through the training, using videos and hands-on techniques to ensure the material is understood.

For employees, a thirty-six-hour hands-on training with qualified staff prepares new hires for the complexities of caring for high-needs infants. Lily's Place provides ongoing training to staff throughout the year to keep them current and up to date.

Our forty-six-point training checklist is provided below.

## Employee Training Checklist

### First Ten Days

- Mission, Goals
- Services/Policies/Procedures
- Organizational Chart

- Continuous Quality Improvement
- Confidentiality/HIPPA
- Mandated Reporting
- Incidents Documentation
- Ethics
- Fire Drill and Safety
- Waste Management
- Medical Emergencies
- Emergency Responses
- Admissions
- Medication Access
- Side Effects of Meds
- Documenting Case Records
- Finger Scanner

## First Thirty Days

- NAS Symptoms
- Management of Sick Babies
- Therapeutic Handling
- Nonjudgment
- First Aid
- Infant CPR
- Medication Reactions/Allergies
- Biohazard/Medical Waste/Infectious Disease
- Security
- Drug Abuse as a Disease
- NAS Effects on Development
- Patient and Family Rights
- Formula Handling
- No-Photo Policy
- Cultural Sensitivity
- Cleaning/Sanitary Methods

- Storage of Cleaning Supplies
- Parenting Skills
- Basic Child Care
- Development and Care of Patients
- Proper Documentation
- Storage of Supplies
- Familial Behavior Management

## First Ninety Days

- Family Dynamics
- Baby Growth and Development
- Management of Aggressive Parents
- Grievances
- Heart Monitor

# Registering with the Board of Pharmacy

Before you can administer medication to your patients, you will need to register and apply to do so with your state's board of pharmacy. For us, the application process was not difficult, but it required a site visit by yet another government official. You cannot register with the US Drug Enforcement Administration until you have obtained a controlled substance permit with your board of pharmacy.

One of the stipulations for us to receive our controlled substance permit was that we engage with a consultant pharmacist—a pharmacist who takes additional courses throughout the year to maintain his or her consultant pharmacist status. A consultant pharmacist can help direct you in the storage and documentation of your medicine so that you meet the strict regulations of the US Drug Enforcement Administration.

A good consultant pharmacist will guide you so that when the board of pharmacy and the DEA actually come for a site visit, all your policies and procedures will be ready and complete. Your controlled substance permit must be renewed yearly.

Our initial consultant pharmacist was a retiree who happily donated his time and talents to us as we applied for the board of pharmacy and DEA permits. He helped us establish our medicine-handling policies and procedures and walked through the building to ensure we were following the appropriate steps.

As the first year of operation progressed, our consultant pharmacist was spending more and more time at his vacation home in North Carolina, and we found that we needed to find another before our board of pharmacy license expired. We paid the applicable fees for a pharmacist at our local compounding pharmacy to become a consultant pharmacist, and we will continue to pay her annual continuing education credits in exchange for her service to Lily's Place.

# Obtaining a DEA Certificate

Once you receive your permit from the state board of pharmacy, obtaining the DEA certificate is easy. You will have already met every requirement except for the application. Your certificate will be good for three years.

# Considering Security

At Lily's Place, we take security very seriously. Nothing is more important to us than the health and safety of our patients and staff. With that said, we recognize that others may want access to the medicine we keep here for the babies, even though the dosages are ridiculously small. We feel that our security system is the best in downtown Huntington.

We employ uniformed security guards and use state-of-the-art video security systems to guarantee the safety of our patients, staff, and parents. One of our video security systems is monitored off-site by security professionals, and Lily's Place staff can access the video stream live from their smartphones. The other system is an in-house video security system with mobile monitors and computer access. Whether inside or outside our property, there are eyes on everyone. In addition to the video security and security guards, we have a cellular-based security alarm system in place that works whether the on-site phones are in operation or not. This security system includes nine panic buttons distributed throughout the building that immediately dispatch the police, who are never more than four blocks from us.

Beyond the alarms, cameras, and human security, our agency's policies are designed for added protection. Each child is allowed only two visitors at a time. One of those visitors must be a parent as listed on that child's birth certificate. At admission, the parent or guardian makes a list of the people who are approved to visit the baby. If a person's name is not on the list of approved visitors, then our security guards deny entry to that individual. We check identification of each visitor prior to entry. No one is allowed in the building unless he or she is credentialed to be inside.

Further, no person may enter the building with a weapon unless he or she is an on-duty police officer responding to a call. No personal belongings are permitted beyond the first set of keypad entry doors except for a set of keys and a cell phone. We have lockers for all personal items, and we strictly enforce this policy.

We have layers of protection in place beyond what is listed here.

# Taking Advantage of Social Media

Social media is your best friend and your worst nightmare. Lily's Place has used social media to garner much-needed community support. Utilizing Facebook, Twitter, YouTube, and our own website, we have built a brand that is recognized in the tristate area and beyond. Once a Facebook admin mused that it would be nice to have flowers planted out front, and just two hours later there was a team of people out front digging, weeding, and planting. Last winter we had a gas bill of over a thousand dollars. We posted the amount on social media, and a man sent us a check for that amount. We have fundraised, advocated, and celebrated through our social media sites.

The downside of social media is the amount of time it takes to administer them effectively. By linking Facebook and Twitter accounts, we cut our time in half, but keeping up with emerging trends; posting relevant content; and keeping up with comments, retweets, and private messages is a big commitment for a small business. The other problem we've had with social media is that we fall under HIPAA requirements, so even though the baby in Room 12 is adorable and has nothing at home for her upon discharge, we simply cannot give out any information or post pictures of our babies. Once, we posted "It's a girl" with no photo, and the state licensure specialist wrote us up for sharing too much information about a patient.

Our advice is to be very careful with regard to social media. As much as you need it, every post you make is scrutinized and criticized.

Please visit our social media sites. Our website is www.lilysplace. org, our Facebook page is www.facebook.com/addictedbabies, and our Twitter site is www.twitter.com/addicted_babies.

# Taking Legislative Action

You may find that your state requires some legislative action for you to be able to operate a facility such as Lily's Place. In the case of Lily's Place, we were a completely new program. There was no template to follow, and state governments do not produce out-of-the-box thinkers. We are an NAS center, so it is logical that we would be licensed as such. However, there was no such designation for us to fall under. We had to adjust ourselves to fit under the regulations of a group home, and we felt that we needed to create a designation that better encompassed who we are. Although the babies live at our facility during the short-term, acute phase of their withdrawal, we are a residential treatment facility for newborns, not a group home. We provide a level of care that is comparable to that of our hospital counterparts, and we needed legislative action to create an appropriate state designation and license.

The process is complicated, but a good-hearted legislator will help you. The first step is to contact your local delegates and senators and schedule a meeting with them when the legislature is *out* of session. Provide them with solid statistics regarding the numbers of NAS cases in your area, and show them photos and examples of what you want to create. These kindhearted legislators will lead you in the right direction as far as what is needed. Do not go into your meeting without doing research, though. Find out possible licensure routes and what is required to be licensed in each way. Find out what statutes are currently in place for similar facilities. Make visits to other facilities, and interview the directors there to learn as much as you can. The more evidence you can provide to your state, the better your chances are of getting appropriate legislation passed.

Then when the legislature is in session, find out who serves on the health and human services committees in each house, and write him or her a letter explaining what you would like to do and that you covet the person's support. Then write very succinctly what you need, and send it to the legislator you met during the off-season who was the most interested in your cause. There are bill writers at the state level who can draft a bill for you. You do not have to be a lawyer to get this done; you just need to know who can help you. Your legislator contacts can be the sponsors of your bill. You can watch the legislative process happen without endangering your nonprofit status. Never pay a legislator or even offer to buy him or her lunch. Doing so is strictly prohibited.

# Creating Partnerships

An important component of starting a residential treatment facility for NAS babies is partners who believe in you and what you are doing. Lily's Place has developed key partnerships that have made our dream a reality. Following is an outline of each of these partnerships.

## WV Department of Health and Human Resources

This is our most valuable partner and greatest resource. The WVDHHR has been supportive of our efforts ever since our company was in its concept phase. The good folks at the state level have reworked existing state code to make it work for NAS babies. They have collaborated with varying agencies and authorities in ways that most would think impossible for any government agency. Cabinet Secretary Karen Bowling and Governor Earl Tomblin have made Lily's Place a priority, from the secretary's desk all the way down to the CPS workers in the field. From Lily's Place's concept to reality, the DHHR has been our best ally.

## Prestera Center

The Prestera Center was an early supporter of Lily's Place, and through an agreement with Prestera CEO Karen Yost, our social worker is a Prestera employee. Having the expertise and resources of the largest substance abuse and mental health provider in the state of West Virginia gives us the peace of mind that our parents will receive the best care. Our social worker provides counseling and support, including connecting families with community service organizations. With Prestera's help, we can connect the abused with help, find shelter for the homeless, provide food for the hungry, and provide clothes for those in need.

## Cabell Huntington Hospital

Early on in our journey, we partnered more formally with Cabell Huntington Hospital (CHH), which wanted to manage the operations side of Lily's Place—and we were happy to let that happen. About four months into the agreement, however, CHH realized that without a significant (in the millions) investment, our facility could not be Centers for Medicare and Medicaid Services (CMS) compliant. Without a variance on hallway width, CHH could not manage our facility. We dissolved the agreement, but we remain the closest of friends. The director of nursing is Lily's Place's greatest friend, offering advice and support. The director of the Hoops Family Children's Hospital at CHH, Bunny Smith, RN worked out an arrangement whereby our first nurses and patient care assistants (PCAs) could train on-site with CHH patients. Clinical Coordinator Sara Murray, RN, who runs the Neonatal Therapeutic Unit at Cabell, is on our board of directors and works with Medical Director Sean Loudin, MD, to identify babies who are candidates for Lily's Place.

## Marshall University Pediatrics

Our medical director, Dr. Sean Loudin, MD; pediatrician Dr. Sherrie Miranda, MD; and our follow-up coordinator, Dr. Mitzi Payne, MD, are all affiliated with Marshall University Pediatrics. Dr. Loudin, a neonatologist, is a regional expert in the care of neonatal abstinence syndrome. All our directives, orders, and protocols are based on his work.

## Valley Health

Through our partnership, the physicians of Valley Health are available to make rounds on our patients, change dosage amounts, and assess and treat the babies at Lily's Place.

## The Medicine Shoppe

Our partnership with The Medicine Shoppe allows for necessary medicine to be delivered within minutes of a baby's admission to Lily's Place. One of the only compounding pharmacies in our area, The Medicine Shoppe actually makes the medicine in the amounts that our tiny patients can tolerate.

## National Alarm

National Alarm provides our fire alarm system, our security system, our panic buttons, and our video monitoring systems.

## Security America

Our partnership with Security America provides daily security guards.

## Abbott

The nutritional needs of our infants are met with products provided by Abbott.

Regional recovery groups and churches have also partnered with us to provide support and services to our families.

# Tips for Clinical Management

Our approach to caring for these babies is one of minimal stress, proper handling, and utilizing an established protocol for weaning when pharmacologic intervention is necessary. Intensive and ongoing training for nurses to ensure all protocols are followed was instituted and is constantly evaluated.

Parents have stated in the past that infants are not always given the appropriate amounts of medication, and studies have shown that infants sent home on methadone require a longer weaning process and are exposed to more medication over time. Thus, we do not send babies home on a weaning dose of methadone.

Our length of stay for opiate-only–exposed babies has dropped significantly and is currently at twenty-one to twenty-five days.

Infants of mothers who abuse multiple drugs continue to present a challenge.

Continuing and intensive education equips parents and caregivers to manage these very complex infants after discharge.

The information on the following pages has been provided by our clinicians to help nurses and physicians as they identify best practices for the care of NAS patients.

# Clinician's Recommendations

## Minimal Stress

To ensure the best environment for recovery, we focus on the following items to reduce stress:

- A low-light, low-stimulus environment
- Slow introduction of stimulus as treatment progresses
- Therapeutic handling using a system developed by Barbara Drennen in Kent, Washington, that controls the movements of the baby and provides specific handling modalities

## Gastric Volume Management

We have developed a volume-driven feeding protocol to decrease gastric overstimulation. Following is an example of this feeding protocol.

### Medical Management of Volume-Driven Feeding
Days 1–6:

- Start feedings at 60 ml/kg/day to 120 ml/kg/day.
- Minimum feeding volume is to be 60 ml/kg/day.
- Daily weights for seven days or until birth weight is regained.

Days 7–13:

- Maximum volume is to be 150 ml/kg/day.
- Minimum volume is to be 120 ml/kg/day.

Our goal is that all infants be at birth weight or greater by day fourteen of life. If the infant has not regained birth weight by day fourteen, we continue to weigh daily and increase feedings to 175 ml/kg/day.

After forty-eight hours of giving the infant the increased volume (175 ml/kg/day), we consider increasing caloric content rather than volume.

The following are approved methods of increasing caloric intake:

- Neosure: 22 calories per ounce
- Similac Expert: 24 calories per ounce
- Protein liquid fortifier: 24 calories per ounce
- Concentrated liquid formula
- Rice Cereal: 1 teaspoon = 5 calories
  - 1 teaspoon rice cereal/60 ml of 20-calorie formula = 22.5 calories per ounce
  - 1½ teaspoons rice cereal/60 ml of 20-calorie formula = 23.75 calories per ounce

The infant should be weighed daily until he or she is consistently gaining weight. Excessive weight gain of more than 30 g/day over a one-week period may allow for a decrease in caloric content. During the seventy-two-hour period after discontinuation of methadone, nurses may consider increasing feedings by 15 ml as needed.

This feeding protocol manages volume and calories to ensure appropriate weight gain while decreasing the amount of gas and regurgitation, which increases scores and prolongs treatment.

## Pharmacologic Intervention
We also developed a weaning protocol that coincides with the scores assessed by using the Finnegan score.

Methadone Weaning Protocol

Our protocols are based on the NAS score using the modified Finnegan score. We initiate pharmacologic therapy for any infant with a score of 8 or greater on three consecutive scores or a score of 12 or greater on two consecutive scores.

We start methadone using a 1 mg/1 ml solution.
- **Step 1:** 0.05 mg/kg Q 6 hours x 48 to 72 hours
    - If scores are greater than 8, after three doses proceed to step 1A.
  - **Step 1A:** 0.05 mg/kg Q 3 hours x 8 doses
    - If average Finnegan scores are still greater than 8 after four doses on step 1A, increase dose by 0.025 mg/kg/dose Q 3 hours x 4 doses until Finnegan score is 8 or lower (e.g., 0.075 mg/kg Q 3 hours x 4 doses, then 0.1 mg/kg Q 3 hours x 4 doses, etc.).
    - Continue dose needed to obtain control for twenty-four hours.
    - If average Finnegan score is lower than 8, wean each day by 0.025 mg/kg/dose until back to 0.05 mg/kg/dose Q 3 hours, and then advance to step 1B.
  - **Step 1B:** 0.05 mg/kg Q 4 hours x 6 doses
  - **Step 1C:** 0.05 mg/kg Q 6 hours x 4 doses
- **Step 2:** 0.04 mg/kg Q 6 hours x 4–8 doses
- **Step 3:** 0.03 mg/kg Q 6 hours x 4–8 doses
- **Step 4:** 0.02 mg/kg Q 6 hours x 4–8 doses
- **Step 5:** 0.25mg/kg Q 8 hours x 3–6 doses
- **Step 6:** 0.02 mg/kg Q 8 hours x 3–6 doses
- **Step 7:** 0.02 mg/kg Q 12 hours x 2–4 doses
- **Step 8:** 0.01 mg/kg Q 12 hours x 2–4 doses
- **Step 9:** 0.01 mg/kg Q 24 hours x 1 dose

Observe infant for seventy-two hours after discontinuing medication; the average Finnegan score should be lower than 8 to wean.

- If the average Finnegan score is 8 to 12, do not wean.
- If the average Finnegan score is greater than 12, go back on taper one step.
- If the average Finnegan score is greater than 12 for forty-eight hours, go back two steps on taper.
- Adjust for weight gain (only once per week) if infant fails to wean after two attempts.

Be sure to educate staff on the interpretation of the Finnegan score so all babies are scored consistently.

## Finnegan Score Interpretation

This is Lily's Place's interpretation in an attempt to be consistent in our scoring

### Crying

This is to be scored only if the infant continues to cry after having been fed, swaddled, held, and having had his or her diaper changed. This describes an inconsolable infant. If the crying continues for less than five minutes, the infant is scored for excessive crying. If the crying continues for more than five minutes, the infant is scored for continuous crying. The cry can be, but does not have to be, high-pitched; however, it does have to be inconsolable. This does not include infants who are crying because they are left unattended.

### Sleeping

This should reflect the longest amount of consistent sleep within the scoring interval. You do not add up the small amounts of sleep to determine the amount; the sleep needs to be consistent. If the infant only stirs or awakens briefly and goes back to sleep, it should not be counted. We want the score to reflect the infant's degree of withdrawal, so we should not score for not sleeping if the infant is awakened by the physician, nurse, or parents or if the baby has a dirty diaper. We also want to take into consideration the infant's age and behavior. If the infant is awake and pleasant without being held or if he or she is a month old and does not require as much sleep and is content while awake, we would not score the infant for not sleeping.

### Moro Reflex

All infants should have a Moro reflex (also known as a startle reflex). You can elicit the reflex by lifting the infant slightly off the mattress by the wrists and allowing him or her to fall back on the mattress or by raising the infant to a sitting position and allowing him or her to fall back into your hand. The reflex consists of a straightening of the arms up and out and the formation of a C shape with the hands. The arms then return to the chest in a flexion or resting position. Extension of the knees and hip joints followed by flexion may also occur. The infant may cry or grimace during this procedure. The infant is scored for hyperactive Moro reflex if he or she repeatedly elicits this response one or two more times after the initial response or during normal movements such as burping or turning. Score for markedly hyperactive Moro reflex if you observe clonus—repetitive, involuntary jerking of the wrist or ankle—of hands and feet after initiation of the reflex.

### Tremors

This should be scored if the infant has involuntary movements of hands, feet, arms, or legs. Tremors are considered mild if they involve only the hands or feet. Tremors are considered moderate to severe if they involve the entire extremity—the arm or leg. Tremors are considered disturbed if they are seen during care or when the infant is being handled. Tremors are considered undisturbed if they are exhibited when the infant is at rest or not being disturbed. Mild tremors do *not* mean the infant tremors only a little or the tremors are not severe. If the tremors involve the whole body, such as shuddering, they would be considered moderate to severe.

## Increased Muscle Tone
Assess muscle tone when the infant is awake and calm. Slowly pull the infant into a sitting position and observe him or her for head lag, rigidity, and arching. Score for increased tone if no head lag is noted, the infant is rigid, or the infant is arching. You should also score for increased tone if flexion of the extremities is tight and you are unable to gently extend the arm or leg.

## Excoriation
This would be scored if there is breakdown of the skin that may be caused by rubbing against the bed linen or blankets or from abnormal stools. Areas most likely to show rubbing excoriation include the chin, knees, cheeks, elbows, toes, and fingers. Acidic and frequent stools may cause excoriation in the diaper area. We score for this every time we see excoriation until it is healing. The area should be broken, raw, or very angry-looking before it is scored, not just red.

## Myoclonic Jerks
These are involuntary spasms of the muscles in the face, arms, and legs that are more pronounced than the jitteriness of tremors. They are irregular, quick, and localized. These movements are most common during sleep and can occur singly or as multiple jerks.

## Generalized Convulsions

These can be described as myoclonic jerks that are more generalized. In a generalized convulsion, more than one extremity is involved. Subtle seizure activity—including rapid, involuntary eye movements, chewing, rowing of the arms, bicycling of the legs, arching of the back, and fist clenching—should also be scored in this category. If the movement is an actual seizure, it will not stop if the extremity is touched or flexed.

## Sweating

This should be scored if there is visible sweat on the infant's head or upper lip or if the infant's hair or clothes are wet with sweat. It should not be scored if the infant is overheated because of being covered with excessive blankets.

## Hyperthermia

The infant is scored 1 if his or her temperature is 99 to 101 degrees Fahrenheit and is scored 2 if his or her temperature is over 101 degrees Fahrenheit. The temperature should be taken when the infant is awakened for assessment, not after the infant has been undressed or diaper changed.

## Frequent Yawning

This can be a sign that the infant is overstimulated and should be scored when the infant yawns three or more times during a scoring interval. The yawning does not have to occur three times in a row, just three times during the scoring interval.

## Mottling

This is a discoloration of the skin that resembles marbling. It is typically seen on the chest, trunk, arms, or legs. It is also often seen if an infant has been uncovered and becomes chilled. This condition should be scored when it is observed unless the caregiver is responsible for the infant being chilled.

## Nasal Stuffiness
This is to be scored if the infant sounds stuffy and has noisy respirations.

## Sneezing
This can also be a sign of overstimulation and should be scored if the infant sneezes three or more times during a scoring interval. As with yawning, this does not have to occur three times in a row, although it can.

## Nasal Flaring
This is the outward spreading of the nostrils during regular breathing, not during feeding. It is normal for infants to do this while sucking a bottle. Score it if observed during normal breathing while the infant is sleeping or resting quietly.

## Respiratory Rate
A normal respiratory rate for an infant is between thirty and sixty breaths per minute. If breathing is labored, you may see retractions. Score 1 if the infant's respiratory rate is greater than sixty, and score 2 if the infant's respiratory rate is greater than sixty with retractions. Respirations should be counted for at least thirty seconds; however, a full minute is preferred.

## Excessive Sucking
We score for excessive sucking if the infant sucks so vigorously on the pacifier or bottle that it is audible or if the baby has to have the pacifier most of the time between feedings to sleep. This is also counted if the infant sucks the bottle so vigorously that he or she is unable to swallow the formula because it is coming out so quickly.

### Poor Feeding

Poor feeding is defined as infrequent or uncoordinated sucking. This should be scored if the infant takes more than thirty minutes to ingest an ounce of formula or if the infant requires lots of stimulation throughout the feeding (e.g., chin/cheek support, bottle manipulation, repositioning of infant).

### Regurgitation

This is scored when the infant has two or more episodes of spitting not associated with burping. This does not include a normal wet burp. Regurgitation of 5 ml or more between feedings should be scored here.

### Projectile Vomiting

This is scored whenever an infant vomits forcefully. This can occur during a feeding or after it. The difference between vomiting and regurgitation relates to the forcefulness of the ejection of stomach contents. Vomiting is the more forceful of the two.

### Loose Stools

This is scored when the infant's stool is curdy, seedy, or runny in appearance. Sometimes the infant's formula may need to be considered if it makes the stools prone to be loose, especially if stools were previously normal.

### Watery Stools

This is scored if stool is liquid in consistency or explosive or if it is surrounded by a water ring, even if it has substance to it.

## Parent Education

All parents are given the opportunity to learn to care for their infant. All parents are required to watch admission and discharge videos;

the videos cover the effects of prenatal substance abuse on the infant brain. All parents are also instructed in infant CPR, are required to view the *Period of PURPLE Crying* video, and are instructed based on the safe sleep initiative. They are educated regarding the scoring and treatment of their infant and are taught therapeutic handling and how to create a lower stimulus environment in their own home. Finally all parents are taught about basic child care prior to discharge.

All of these interventions must be coordinated and evaluated continuously as we attempt to provide the best treatment and opportunities for our babies to go home healthy and to a safe environment.

We do and will always strive to be the voice for the baby.

# A Sample Business Plan

## Lily's Place
A Pediatric Residential Treatment Facility for Drug-Exposed Newborns

## I. Organizational Summary

Lily's Place is chartered as a nonprofit 501(c)(3) corporation in Huntington, West Virginia, with the goal of providing observation and therapeutic and pharmacologic care to infants suffering from prenatal drug exposure. As we heal the infant, our goal is to connect families with recovery groups and available resources to improve the life of the baby once he or she is discharged from our facility. Lily's Place provides training to parents and caregivers, connects them with appropriate services, and mentors and assists the state with babies as complex social issues arise within families. We are located at 1320 Seventh Avenue in Huntington, West Virginia. The building is a former podiatrist's office, was donated by Laura Darby, and was accepted by Lily's Place Inc. on June 12, 2013.

Our medical director, Sean Loudin, MD, is one of the most respected neonatologists in our area who specializes in the care of drug-exposed babies. His oversight allows NAS expert Rhonda Edmunds, RN, and her staff to safely wean the prenatally exposed babies from the effects of their mothers' drugs while providing them with a nurturing environment in which to recover. Additionally, the staff at

Lily's Place works with social workers and CPS to educate and support parents as they bond with their babies and begin their own journeys to end chemical dependence.

Our board of directors has been carefully selected from concerned citizens in the Huntington area. The board meets quarterly to review progress and steer our staff toward the achievement of our main objectives. The board's executive committee meets monthly to work toward meeting short-term goals, also overseeing the finances of Lily's Place.

# 2. Getting Started

## 2.1 What Makes Lily's Place Unique

Although the hospital model of care practiced across the country provides babies withdrawing from drugs with physician oversight and nursing care, the doctors and nurses assigned to the drug-exposed babies are usually not trained in therapeutic handling techniques.

An added problem is the limited number of beds for critically ill babies, and because the average drug-exposed baby requires four to six weeks of care, our region's specially trained neonatologists are in a tough position. They cannot turn away drug-exposed babies, but their neonatal intensive care units were designed for intensive, not therapeutic, care. There simply is not enough space in the neonatal intensive care unit to supply beds for both critically ill babies and babies with neonatal abstinence syndrome. The answer is clear: keep the critically ill babies where they belong, in the intensive care units, and refer drug-exposed babies to a group residential facility for NAS babies, such as Lily's Place.

Lily's Place director of nursing, Rhonda Edmunds, RN, is a national leader in the complex treatment and therapeutic handling techniques necessary to wean babies from the medication used to treat their withdrawal symptoms and get them back on the right path for healing and developmental growth. She and her staff all have specialized training in caring for drug-exposed infants.

Lily's Place is the only place of its kind in the United States and will serve as a model for other communities that recognize the emerging crisis of substance-abused infants, and we are the only place that offers help and support to families. We are truly one of a kind.

## 2.2 Legal Entity

Lily's Place is chartered as a nonprofit 501(c)(3) corporation in Huntington, West Virginia. Its board of directors has been carefully drawn from the local medical communities and from concerned citizens.

## 2.3 Start-up Summary

### Start-up Expenses

A major hurdle to opening the doors at Lily's Place was the high cost of creating a medical facility from the ground up. Combining community support and much-needed grant money, we have been able to meet every fiscal need thus far. In addition to minor building modifications (including a $50,000 sprinkler system, which has been purchased and installed), a $30,000 generator (purchased and installed), a fire alarm system, and office expenses (including computers, purchased accounting and donor software, donated copiers, and the requisite list of supplies necessary to start a business), we also needed medical equipment, including heart/blood pressure monitors, masks, thermometers, and blood pressure cuffs (all purchased and on-site). In addition to those necessary business and medical items, we needed all the comforts parents need when they bring their babies home from the hospital, including baby beds (donated), swings (donated), rocking chairs (donated), baby clothes (donated), bottles, diapers (mounds of diapers), baby wipes (donated), burping cloths (donated), blankets (donated), shampoo (donated), lotion (donated), and all the little things that bring comfort to a sick baby. We also required a few major items, including a washer and dryer (both donated), a high-tech video and alarm system (installed), a new air conditioner (purchased with donations and installed), and a secure location to store medicine (done), which is administered in lower and lower doses until the baby is no longer chemically dependent.

As is clear from the above list, the community has poured out its heart and dug into its pockets to help us secure all of our start-up needs.

### Start-up Assets

Lily's Place has been blessed by a donation of a nearly perfect building from a local family who is passionate about helping these sick babies. The building is approximately 7,250 square feet, with sixteen rooms that have been converted into nurseries, four bathrooms, two furnace rooms, two large storage rooms, four small washrooms, a staff break room, four private offices, a laundry room, two closets, one very large, open office space, and a waiting room. The building is in excellent condition and has passed very rigorous state fire marshal licensure requirements.

The building belongs to Lily's Place Inc. without any lien on the property, free and clear. The property was assessed at $500,000 in summer 2014. Additionally, we have donated cash available to pay employees, and reimbursements have started rolling in. We are grateful that so far we have not borrowed a single penny.

### Furnishings

Each of the sixteen nurseries already has one or two baby beds, depending on the size of the room. Smaller rooms will be reserved as singles for those babies in the greatest distress. We anticipate three single rooms, and the remaining will be double-occupancy rooms. We now have twenty-nine baby beds, twenty-nine tables or cabinets for storage in the rooms, twenty-nine regular side tables, and thirty-five rocking chairs in addition to bedding and therapeutic tools. Each room has a fire-resistant rug to muffle sound, donated by caring members of the community. Currently under our initial license, we can accept twelve babies, and each baby has his or her own room.

I strongly encourage you to visit our website at www.lilys-place.org and to take a virtual tour at https://www.youtube.com/watch?v=9LvX96uAsi8 to view our facility. I promise it will be worth your time.

### Funding

To fund these start-up costs, our board president was able to arrange for Lily's Place to receive $50,000 in start-up money from Governor Tomblin through a BHHF grant. A $9,711 grant from the March of Dimes was secured to fund the creation of our education center, and we worked with Narcotics Anonymous, Alcoholics Anonymous, and the Prestera Center to stock the education center with materials for adult recovery. We also have a TV and DVD player purchased with donations and set up for recovery and training videos. A grant from a local foundation paid for our generator and our video security system. The city of Huntington awarded us a $250 microgrant, and we have received grants from a local family foundation, the Francis

Foundation, the Foundation for the Tri-State Community, the Lafon Family Foundation, and the Pilot Club of Huntington. We have also received significant donations from individuals and community groups. We've had an outpouring from the community and church groups to decorate nurseries and provide us with everything from medical gloves to pacifiers. In fact, all our rooms were "adopted" by individuals and groups who furnished and decorated them, completing them September 15, 2013. We feel this is yet another major way in which our community has shown support for Lily's Place. Now that we are open, we are billing Medicaid and the WVDHHR for each baby's room, board, and care.

## 2.4 Locations and Facilities

Our spacious outer room serves as the center for parental education. Weekly parenting classes, addiction recovery groups, and faith-based support services occupy this comfortable space. A private counseling office has been created for private consultations with families to determine their specific needs and to try to connect these families with programs and community support as needed. We allow parents and caregivers to use this space as a place to rest and regroup, as days with their infants can be trying.

Beyond our second set of locked doors are sixteen nurseries. Each room is beautifully decorated by community groups, church groups, and individuals who donated their time, expertise, and supplies to make each nursery look as though it were ripped from the pages of a design magazine. Each baby has his or her own crib, storage table, and rocking chair for Mom.

Just outside the nurseries is a nurse's station where the attending registered nurse (RN) charts each baby's progress and makes him- or herself available to babies or parents who need attention when nurses are not giving direct therapeutic care in one of their assigned rooms. Patient care assistants (PCAs) and volunteers are assigned to specific patients to help in the care of each baby.

Security officers keep records of all who enter our building, as well as how long they stay and when they leave. A large, open office space with ample filing and record-keeping capabilities houses the business office. Records are maintained as to which parents have completed their mandatory parenting courses and who has been trained in infant CPR, among other necessary components for the release of infants to their caregivers.

A high-security, monitored space has been designated as the location for storage of medicines and baby formula, while other ample storage areas are where diapers, gowns, baby clothes, and other nursery necessities are stored. Our kitchen area serves as both a break room for our nurses and staff and a board room for our quarterly meetings. Our laundry room has a washer/dryer hookup for the armloads of laundry that accompany up to twenty-nine newborns under one roof. Four small washrooms serve as places for caregivers to bathe the babies.

Our location in Huntington, West Virginia, is a short forty-five minutes from Charleston. We are just an hour from Logan, an hour and a half from Beckley, and two and a half hours from the Lewisburg/Greenbrier area. Our city borders both southern Ohio and eastern Kentucky. Huntington is home to West Virginia's second-largest university, multiple nursing schools, two hospitals, and one medical school. Our location on Seventh Avenue is within four blocks of the city police department, bus depot, and city mission. We are within seven blocks of one of the region's few neonatal intensive care units and an Amtrak station. Our building is accessible from the city bus line, and we are located directly across the street from the area food bank. The population of our region is predominantly lower income, and the city in which we operate is culturally diverse.


## 3. Services

### 3.1 Services Narrative

When a baby is born with drugs in his or her system, he or she is immediately referred to CPS. Physicians evaluate the child to ensure there are no additional medical conditions that can mimic or mask drug withdrawal. Once that determination is made, the baby is transported to Cabell Huntington Hospital's designated unit for neonatal abstinence syndrome or to another NICU within the state. There the baby is started on methadone to control symptoms of withdrawal. Once the baby has been determined to be stable in his or her wean and is tolerating the protocol for withdrawal, he or she is transferred to Lily's Place. Many hospitals don't have an NAS unit, or that unit is filled to capacity. In this case, the drug-affected baby is referred to Cabell Huntington Hospital prior to being transferred to Lily's Place. Babies may also be sent to Lily's Place for observation or in the case of complex social issues that may require a temporary foster situation.

When babies are transported to our group residential facility, they are first examined to see where they fall within the scoring system. Once their initial score is determined, our medical director and registered nurses determine a method of treatment. In nearly all cases, the course of treatment follows the protocols set up by the medical director at Cabell Huntington Hospital, who also serves as Lily's Place's medical director.

Some babies are simply observed, while many others are prescribed weaning doses of medicine to manage the withdrawal. Lily's

Place was specifically designed to fit the needs of a calm and nurturing environment to help ease the pain of withdrawal. Drug-affected babies have heightened senses so that even normal amounts of light and sound can cause great discomfort. Some babies cannot manage to suck on a bottle. Some cannot bear to be touched but need some kind of soothing. Still other babies crave being held. A plan of care is developed for each infant.

Staff members make great efforts to include parents and guardians in the care of their infants. Lily's Place offers scheduled times in which parents can and should spend time with their babies. We offer parenting classes, CPR classes, information on adult addiction recovery, referrals to reputable programs in our area, and state and pastoral care, if requested. Parents are required to participate in our twenty-one-point education program prior to discharge. Our goal is to help the baby, and we understand our time with each baby is limited. Ultimately, the best help for the baby is a parent who is committed to ending his or her own drug dependence. We have currently built partnerships with reputable names such as Prestera, Project Hope, Renaissance, Healing Place, Oasis, Cabell County Substance Abuse Prevention Program, and others to connect mothers and fathers with appropriate help. Additionally, we are working with the Huntington Food Bank, Every Little Bottom, Birth to Three, Success by Six, and the Cabell County Family Resource Network to ensure mothers know what services are available to help their babies. We are developing relationships with other groups and physicians to help follow up with our babies after they are discharged. Much research is needed to learn how prenatal drug abuse affects the developing brain, and what (if any) lingering effects this exposure has on the child as he or she enters the school system. We are eager to help research teams follow these children who often fall through the cracks due to changing contact numbers and residences. We conduct a follow-up clinic to provide a system in which mothers check in at Lily's Place for free diapers and other donated supplies, helping to keep track of these high-risk children.

As the infants are weaned from their medications, the skilled nursing staff continues to score the infants to determine how well they are coping. Higher scores indicate a more distressed baby, while lower scores indicate a return toward normal newborn behavior. Medicine and care are adjusted accordingly. The ultimate goal is a baby who has been drug-free for seventy-two hours and scores in the normal range. This process can take anywhere from two to six weeks.

When a baby has been off medicine for seventy-two hours, Lily's Place often invites the child's mother, grandmother, caregiver, or foster parent to room-in with the baby for twenty-four to forty-eight hours. This kind of hands-on training is valuable for the person who will ultimately care for the baby. With two days of supervised on-the-job training, we feel confident that the baby's caregiver will be trained and ready for what lies ahead in the days and weeks to come. This rooming-in period also gives our social worker and CPS valuable data about how the mother copes with caring for a high-stress infant.

Should the mother decide at any time that parenting the child will not fit into her lifestyle, Lily's Place staff will be there to help her through the process.

In some cases, after a baby has gone home from the hospital with her parent, CPS determines in a follow-up visit to remove that child from the home and put him or her in foster care. Babies born with NAS are very difficult to care for, and a specific kind of foster situation is required for these high-needs babies. Lily's Place can be a temporary foster for these babies until appropriate placements are found. At Lily's Place, we feel strongly that appropriate care and handling can make a difference in the life of a child. We welcome these temporary fosters and give them the love and nurture they need as they develop.

Lily's Place works with the WVDHHR and Pressley Ridge to act as a location for information sessions about becoming foster parents for NAS babies. Additionally, we are registered as a diaper bank with the National Diaper Bank Network, and we collect and provide diapers to clothing pantries in the Huntington area and to the Huntington City Mission.

## 3.2 Alternative Providers

There are a few alternatives for the kind of care Lily's Place provides. One, of course, is to keep the baby at the hospital for the withdrawal period. This poses several problems. First, most hospitals are not equipped or designed to keep newborns for the length of time necessary to properly wean them from the drugs in their systems. Hospitals with neonatal intensive care units have a limited number of beds for critically ill babies. With this epidemic of drug-exposed infants, hospitals do not have room to care for the overwhelming number of babies for this extended period of time. In addition, the cost of keeping a baby for up to six weeks or longer in a hospital setting is exorbitant. Especially in West Virginia, where poverty is the norm, our state is footing the bill in many cases for these chemically dependent patients.

There are many alternative ways to care for drug-exposed neonates. The key is to find the method that best fits the population you are serving. Our model fits the needs of the Huntington, West Virginia, area.

Lily's Place offers the highest level of care in a nurturing, home-like environment twenty-four hours a day, seven days a week, until each baby is ready to be released. Parents are supervised and trained to help ease the discomfort of their infants.

## 3.3 Printed Materials and Media

We distribute postcards with bullet points and brochures for parents, hospitals, and clinics, describing the services we offer.

Our fundraising packet will soon be completed, with photos of our beautiful facility and testimonials from parents who have experienced what Lily's Place has to offer.

We encourage you to visit our website at www.lilysplace.org to read about our journey and the creation of Lily's Place. Please visit our contact page so we can send you additional information.

Lily's Place also maintains a Facebook page (www.facebook.com/addictedbabies), a Twitter account (www.twitter.com/addicted_babies), and other necessary social media property as a way to educate others about what we do and in hope that other folks will create similar organizations. Please watch this brief video tour, created by local high school students: https://www.youtube.com/watch?v=9LvX96uAsi8.

As for media coverage, all three television stations in our area, WOWK-TV, WSAZ-TV, and WCHS/FOX-TV, have done segments on Lily's Place. The *Herald-Dispatch*, the *Ashland Daily Independent*, the *Charleston Gazette*, and the *Daily Mail* have all run articles about our efforts. We have been contacted by ABC News (*Nightline*) for a story after our pilot licensing period ends.

## 3.4 Technology

We have outsourced our billing and payroll to MPMS in Barboursville, West Virginia, coordinating our patient records to best interface with those of our billing vendor. We have received five donated antiquated computers, and one major need we face is to update our computers. We currently use paper charting, but we hope to upgrade to electronic records designed specifically to comply with the Health

Insurance Portability and Accountability Act (HIPAA). Additionally, Lily's Place utilizes QuickBooks, the recommended accounting and donor-tracking software, to maintain accurate financial and tax-reporting records. We are working with Hess, Stewart & Campbell in Huntington to create and maintain appropriate tax records. Our cost reporting is done through Arnett, Foster, & Toothman in Charleston.

Lily's Place is very proud of our plans for ongoing staff training, which will utilize the latest technology. Marshall University and other local schools have contacted us and asked that we set up an internship program, and a good number of nursing students at St. Mary's School of Nursing have indicated an interest in participating in an extern program we hope to start once we have been open two full years.

## 3.5 Future Services

We fully expect Lily's Place to be a model for the care, treatment, and respect of drug-exposed newborns nationwide. Our plan is to welcome infants from across the state and region, to train others with hearts for these babies, and to share our story with anyone who will listen so that Lily's Place can be duplicated. We have been visited by a number of groups who want to replicate our work. This makes us very proud.

Unlike other neonatal abstinence providers, we work with both parent and child; the states of West Virginia, Ohio, and Kentucky; and foster parents, grandparents, and caregivers. Our work is not complete if we release a baby into the care of someone who is unable to care for him- or herself. Our focus is on the health of the baby, and we believe the future health of the child depends strongly on the health of the caregiver.

Within five years, we hope to be the voice for the effective treatment of neonatal abstinence syndrome in our community, state, and nation. We hope to grow our private-sector support base through corporate alliances and grants to help eliminate the need for state assistance outside the roles Medicaid and the WVDHHR play in reimbursing us for the direct care of needy children.

We believe Lily's Place will be a training ground for nurses with a heart for substance-exposed infants. In fact, we welcome those who want to learn to best care for "our" babies.

Additionally, we are working with physicians at Marshall University to create the first ever long-term study of this population of infants. We are working with the National Diaper Bank Network as we establish ourselves as a diaper bank to help stock local food and clothing pantries in the Huntington area.

## 4. Market Analysis

We are basing our market analysis on 2010 census data from Huntington, West Virginia, but please keep in mind that Huntington is the second-largest city in our state. Surrounding regions have similar drug dependence with smaller populations and often lower incomes. Our city is a regional medical magnet for these outlying areas.

### 4.1 Base Numbers

Huntington, West Virginia, has a population of 49,138 people. The larger region including Ashland, Kentucky, and Ironton, Ohio, brings the metropolitan area to 287,702. In Huntington proper, the median income is $23,234 per year. Currently 24.7 percent of all residents of Huntington are below the poverty line. In addition, 29.8 percent of those under nineteen years of age fall below the poverty line.

According to statistics from one hospital in Huntington, 194 babies were identified as having been born exposed to a drug in 2012. Those numbers were much higher for 2013. According to American

Academy of Pediatrics, the national statistical trend of babies diagnosed with neonatal abstinence syndrome is rising sharply. In most communities, five babies per thousand births are drug exposed. In our community, the number of drug-exposed newborns was a whopping 75 births per 1,000 in 2012. That number increased to 108 per 1,000 live births in 2013.

Maternal drug use includes marijuana, cocaine, hallucinogens, heroin, methamphetamines, nonmedical use of prescription drugs, heavy drinking, and tobacco use. A sad statistic from the American Academy of Pediatrics shows that most pregnant women use fewer drugs while pregnant than their nonpregnant peers, but young girls between the ages of fifteen and seventeen have higher usage rates. When you consider that West Virginia and Kentucky have two of the highest rates of teenage pregnancy, with 44.8 and 46.2 births per thousand teenage girls, respectively, you can begin to understand the scope of the infant addiction problem we face.

## 4.2 Market Segmentation
As we see it, our market includes two very different segments of the population: the insured and the uninsured. We currently receive our reimbursements from Medicaid and WVDHHR. As we move into our second year of operations, those babies with insurance will be welcomed and billed at rates that are comparable with those of the ones who depend on the state for their health care. As the Affordable Care Act (Obamacare) changes, our billing processes also will need to adapt. We have worked closely with the Department of Health and Human Resources to create Lily's Place, and we feel confident in their dedication to the care of every baby in West Virginia.

## 4.3 Length of Stay
The length of stay varies considerably depending on the various prenatal exposures. Lily's Place is dedicated to caring for drug-exposed infants and providing the highest quality of care, following

established protocols to guide care. The fact remains that these babies require care that ranges from days to months.

## 4.4 Market Trends

Currently every drug-exposed newborn is referred to CPS. At the point of referral, the WVDHHR becomes involved. We believe that once a baby is determined to be free of all medical conditions unrelated to drug exposure, the best place for that baby is not among the hustle and bustle of a hospital but in a nurturing, quiet, and loving homelike environment—Lily's Place.

We commend one local hospital for creating a unit specifically for NAS babies. Cabell Huntington Hospital has done more for NAS babies than any other medical facility in our state. We work closely with Cabell Huntington Hospital as we form alliances in the care for these tiny victims of drug abuse.

We recognize that parents will have a choice as to where their babies should stay, and we feel strongly that pediatricians, parents, and caregivers will choose the expertise and nurture that is Lily's Place. Not only are we the best choice for the baby, but we go the extra mile for each family we serve.

## 4.5 Market Needs

Clearly, West Virginia (and the nation as a whole) needs an alternative to expensive, hospital-based NAS treatment. We feel we are the model for that alternative.

Whereas the stereotypical drug addict is what comes to mind when we mention the addicted mother, it is important for the public to realize that there is no stereotype for drug addiction. Our mothers are both college educated and high school dropouts. They live both at the city mission and in beautiful homes overlooking our city. They are both college and high school students. Some are addicted to medicine prescribed by their physicians. Some buy and sell drugs on the street. Some of them are so embarrassed to admit they are addicted that they lie to their families about what is wrong with their newborns.

As diverse as the population of addicted mothers is, there are a few things they all have in common.

- They love their babies.
- They want the best medical care for their babies.
- They want to be treated with dignity and respect.
- They want to be active in the care of their children.
- They want their babies to come home.
- They want peace of mind about how their babies will withdraw.

The huge, often unstated elephant in the room is the guilt that most mothers experience knowing that their addiction has significantly affected their newborn babies. At Lily's Place, we offer hope to the guilt-ridden mother. We offer her a listening ear and a chance to make a change. When you look into the eyes of a contrite mother who is desperate in her desire to alter her life for the better as a result of the birth of her child, huge strides can be made to change two lives at once. These connections are not made in a clinical hospital setting. They happen one-on-one.

## 4.6 Partners

At Lily's Place, we stand proud of our partners. We work with pediatricians, our legislators, Cabell Huntington Hospital, Prestera, the Department of Health and Human Resources, CPS, the state of West Virginia, the city of Huntington and its employees, and the drug prevention and family connection groups mentioned previously. We believe that with their continued support, we will be able to provide cutting-edge therapeutic care to our infants. We are indebted to our community and local churches for donating the incredible number of diapers and wipes we need daily. Additionally, local churches and concerned citizens have donated their time, supplies, and talents to make each of our nurseries simply beautiful. As we move forward, we plan to partner with foundations and grants to provide necessary income. We also need to recognize our police department and our chief of police for all they do to keep us safe.

## 4.7 Alternatives and Usage Patterns

Families choose one medical care facility over another for a variety of reasons. The most common issues involved in their decision are distance from their home, affordability, quality of staff and facilities, and medical needs necessary for their baby. Parents usually choose the highest level of care at the most reasonable price within forty-five minutes to an hour of their homes.

## 4.8 Similar NAS Facilities

To our knowledge, there is only one other facility similar to Lily's Place in the United States. The Pediatric Interim Care Center (PICC) in Kent, Washington, is the pioneer in drug-abused infant care. The PICC has helped drug-exposed babies withdraw from chemical dependence since the 1980s. Our staff has met with PICC creator, Barbara Drennen, and created Lily's Place using her advice.

Where PICC differs is that it is basically a foster home. PICC works only with babies who are wards of the state. At Lily's Place, we work with the whole family, and we feel it's a better plan of care for our state, our community, and the family.

# 5. Management

## 5.1 Caregiving Management

Medical Director Sean Loudin, MD, is the ultimate decision maker at Lily's Place. Director of Nursing Rhonda Edmunds is an RN with over twenty-five years of experience and collaborates with Dr. Loudin to prepare reports for the board of directors.

The nursing staff (one RN per six babies) reports to the director of nursing. The PCAs (one PCA per three babies) also report to the director of nursing.

The social worker, secretary, and security officers report to the executive director, as do all hired consultants. Once each quarter, the executive director reports to the board of directors. The volunteer coordinator reports to the executive director, and volunteers report to the volunteer coordinator.

## 5.2 Personnel Plan

Our personnel plan reflects our commitment to offering employment that is meaningful and also compensates our employees fairly for the time, energy, and emotional toil it takes to spend their days caring for crying babies.

To meet our staffing goals, we have hired the following medical and caregiving staff:

- One medical director (providing his oversight pro bono)
- One director of nursing
- Thirteen RNs
- Nine PCAs
- One social worker

We also have the following administrative and development personnel:

- One executive director
- One secretary
- Two security guards
- One volunteer coordinator

# Authors' Note

"Children are the living messages we send to a time we will not see," Neil Postman wrote in the introduction to *The Disappearance of Childhood*. We are obligated as a society to ensure our future by nurturing our children and providing them with the best start possible.

If you are reading this book, you are a human cut from a different pattern. You have made the decision to embrace women and children that the world shuns. Chances are you are struggling to provide the best care to infants who are truly inconsolable.

We invite you to take a deep breath and know that we are your partners, and we will help. Call us with your questions at 304-523-5459. E-mail us with your concerns at information@lilysplace.org. Visit our website at www.lilysplace.org. Follow us on Facebook and Twitter at www.facebook.com/addictedbabies and www.twitter.com/addicted_babies. We hope you will collaborate at www.facebook.com/neonatalabstinencesyndromealliance.

Together we can make a difference in the lives of these babies, and they will become the living messages we send to a time we will not see.

Mary Calhoun Brown, Cofounder
Lily's Place

CPSIA information can be obtained
at www.ICGtesting.com
Printed in the USA
BVHW041551250422
635283BV00009B/873

9 781511 864251